SOUND TRACKS

Blues

Bob Brunning

Heinemann LIBRARY

CONTENTS

On these discs is a selection of the artist's recordings. Many of these albums are now available on CD. If they are not, many of the tracks from them can be found on compilation CDs.

Blues star Bo Diddley with his unique box-shaped guitar.

These boxes give you extra information about the artists and their times.
Some contain anecdotes about the artists themselves or about the people who helped their careers or, occasionally, about those who exploited them.
Others provide historical facts about the music, lifestyle, fans, fads and fashions of the day.

INTRODUCTION

Blues has been entertaining and inspiring listeners for just under a century. Its roots can be traced back to the 1920s and '30s in the deep South of the United States. The black population still suffered terrible deprivation and savage racism, despite the fact that slavery had been abolished several decades before.

Huddie 'Leadbelly' Ledbetter was discovered in prison by Alan Lomax (see page 25), while serving a sentence for murder. He managed to sing his way out, by writing a song for the governor of Texas, pleading for a pardon. He repeated this feat a few years later in a Louisiana prison!

In earlier times, exhausted slaves would comfort themselves by expressing their feelings in music. Farm labourers would often sing songs to the rhythm of their back-breaking tasks, to help them cope with the tedium of the work. Rare free time was enlivened by social gatherings, where workers could relax by eating, drinking and entertaining one another with sorrowful songs, bewailing their fate.

However, by the 1930s and '40s, many talented performers had decided that there might be an audience for their music in the big cities. Musicians such as John Lee Hooker, Elmore James, Muddy Waters, Howlin' Wolf, Bo Diddley, Little Walter, B.B. King and hundreds more made the trips to Chicago and Memphis. The lucky ones were rewarded with fame, if not great fortune. The message spread to Europe and blues music influenced a whole host of bands and musicians in the 1960s. The Rolling Stones, the Yardbirds, Fleetwood Mac, Eric Clapton, Led Zeppelin and the Who all acknowledged their American blues heroes. This support from the most popular musicians of the day encouraged millions of young listeners to explore authentic American blues – many first-generation blues musicians suddenly started enjoying the success they had deserved for years.

It's important to remember that blues music is still with us today, kept alive in clubs and concert halls all over the world. Support and enjoy it!

BIG BILL BROONZY

Big Bill Broonzy was born in Mississippi in 1893. Brought up in a farming community, he endured segregation, racism and poverty, but discovered that he could express his feelings in music in a powerful and moving way. Bill's first instrument was the violin, but he soon found that he could write and accompany himself more successfully on the guitar.

Big Bill was an early blues guitar hero.

'The Young Big Bill Broonzy' 1991

'Where The Blues Began' 2000, recorded 1928–46

WARTIME

Big Bill Broonzy's army service in France during World War One made him realize that there was a bigger world out there, where black people could gain respect and prosperity. On his return to the USA, he went to Chicago and started playing and recording with a number of contemporary blues artists.

FINGER PICKIN' GOOD

He also had a talent for playing jazz – a musical genre closely related to the blues – and by the late 1920s Bill was recording with small jazz groups in and around the Chicago area. Big Bill's superb finger picking style (playing by plucking the strings with his fingers rather than with a plectrum, or 'pick'), his expressive voice and his poignant songs soon brought him to the attention of ever wider audiences.

BIG BILL BLUES

In 1927, Bill had his first hit. Recorded by Paramount, it sold almost exclusively to black enthusiasts. 'Big Bill Blues' helped to put Broonzy on the musical map, and he started recording prolifically with many performers.

SPIRIT OF THE BLUES

A solo appearance at John Hammond's prestigious 'Spiritualists to Swing' concert in 1938 saw Bill harking back to the traditional musical roots from which he had come. His subsequent huge success in Europe on the back of that 'country blues boy' image tended to obscure the wide and diverse contribution he made to the blues. He wrote many classic songs including 'Key To The Highway', 'All By Myself' and 'Wee Wee Hours' which would later be recorded by major blues artists.

FATHER OF THE BLUES

Often known as the 'father of the blues', W.C. Handy was born in Alabama in 1873. He started out playing the cornet with touring bands, and it was during his travels that he first heard primitive blues music. Handy was the first person to publish a tune with the word 'blues' in it – 'Memphis Blues' in 1912. 'Beale Street Blues' and 'Yellow Dog Blues' followed. A movie of his life, 'St Louis Blues' was released in 1958, the year of his death.

A plaque marks the spot where W.C. Handy lived in Clarksdale, Mississippi.

Big Bill died in 1958, just as his music was being discovered by young white musicians.

ALBERT COLLINS

Albert Collins was brought up in Texas, and started his musical career there, playing keyboards in the late 1960s. He relocated to California, switched to guitar and teamed up with the renowned American blues/rock band Canned Heat, and made several albums.

'Ice Pickin'' 1978

'Showdown' 1985, with Robert Cray and Johnny Copeland

'Deluxe Edition' 1997

ICE COOL

Going solo, Albert developed his trademark 'ice cool' guitar style – every album title reflected this theme: 'Frostbite', 'Frozen Alive', 'Cold Snap' and 'Ice Man', for example.

LIVE AID

Albert's career continued to flourish through the 1970s, '80s and '90s. He recorded and toured relentlessly, often in collaboration with other blues stars, such as John Lee Hooker and B.B. King. In 1985, Albert played before the biggest audience of his life – he was one of the few blues musicians to be invited to play at the monumental 'Live Aid' charity concert. His performance with slide guitar hero George Thorogood was seen by a TV audience of 2 billion.

Unusually, Collins hangs his guitar over his right shoulder.

ROBERT CRAY

Robert Cray was born in Georgia, but he spent most of his childhood accompanying his military family all over the United States and Germany. Growing up in the 1960s, Robert listened to a huge number of rock, blues and soul artists. He would skilfully weave all those diverse influences into his later work.

Robert Cray plays the ever-popular Fender Stratocaster guitar.

FATE LENDS A HAND

Robert was a huge fan of Albert Collins, and fate intervened when Albert played at Robert's high school graduation ball. Robert was bowled over by Albert's precise, ice-pickin' style, and along with his friend, bass player Richard Cousins, he talked his way into the Albert Collins band. Robert learned a great deal from Albert over the next two years, and Albert much appreciated Robert's beautiful, soul-tinged voice.

Many critics think that Cray is more accomplished on stage than on record.

SOLO SUCCESS

Robert went solo in 1975 – his album 'Strong Persuader' is one of the biggest-selling blues albums ever. He and Albert joined forces again in 1985 for a monster album, 'Showdown'.

'Who's Been Talkin'' 1980
'Strong Persuader' 1986
'Don't Be Afraid Of The Dark' 1988
'Take Your Shoes Off' 1999

BUDDY GUY

Legend has it that when George 'Buddy' Guy made the trek to Chicago in search of fame and fortune, times were so hard that he practically starved to death. However, blues star Muddy Waters heard about his skills, gave him food to eat and helped to start his long career.

EARLY YEARS

Buddy was born in 1936 in Louisiana. Like so many bluesmen before him, he was brought up in a farming community. He roamed around the South, before making the move to the home of urban blues, Chicago, Illinois.

THE CHESS YEARS

Eventually he was signed to Leonard Chess's label. As he searched for his own voice, he developed a high-energy, heavy version of the blues.

Buddy Guy started out as a sideman for other musicians.

Buddy was cautious during his stint with Chess, hanging on to his day job. This was a wise move, because his career was slow to blossom, but he was persistent, optimistic and worked hard at his craft.

Buddy Guy in concert at London's Royal Festival Hall.

'The Complete Chess Studio Recordings' 1992, recorded 1960–67
'Damn Right, I've Got The Blues' 1991
'Buddy's Blues' 1997
'Buddy's Baddest' 1999, recorded 1991–99

FAMOUS FRIENDS

After his time at Chess, Buddy made some excellent albums with harmonica player Junior Wells, and started to make waves in Europe on the burgeoning festival scene. His flamboyant approach certainly suited a big stage with massive amplification. Things went a bit quiet on the recording front for a while, until Silvertone signed him in the early 1990s. Buddy recorded the fine album 'Damn Right I've Got The Blues', featuring UK heroes Mark Knopfler, Jeff Beck and Eric Clapton, who is a big fan of Buddy. Other successful albums followed, including 'Heavy Love' and 'Real Deal'.

TRIBUTE

He continues to tour the world, often paying musical tributes to the blues giants of the past. But Buddy Guy is a fine and original bluesman in his own right, who has influenced a new generation of musicians.

ERIC CLAPTON

The most successful blues musician of all time was not born in America's deep South, but in the south of England. Eric Clapton only took up the guitar in his late teens, but within two years he was the hottest player in London. Eric was the star of the Yardbirds, John Mayall's Bluesbreakers, Cream, Blind Faith and Derek and the Dominoes, before he launched a solo career which has lasted for over 30 years.

Eric Clapton learns some licks from Buddy Guy.

JOHN LEE HOOKER

Along with B.B. King, John Lee Hooker was one of the last surviving Mississippi bluesmen who made the journey to the northern cities in the 1930s and '40s. Twenty years later, his music was embraced by white pop musicians, who recorded his songs and brought him the international fame he deserved. Unintentionally, he changed the face of modern music, helping to give it the blues roots which can still be heard today.

John Lee Hooker, pictured in the 1990s.

CLARKSDALE TO DETROIT

John Lee Hooker was born in Clarksdale, Mississippi in 1920. His stepfather, an accomplished guitarist, encouraged him to play the blues, and taught him the guitar by the time he was twelve. In the late 1930s, John Lee migrated – but not to Chicago like so many other bluesmen. He went first to Memphis, and ended up in Detroit in 1943.

On stage with Carlos Santana.

BOOGIE MAN

John Lee was given his first electric guitar in 1947 by the legendary Texan bluesman T. Bone Walker. During the day, he worked as a janitor in a car factory, and by night he performed in blues clubs. Gradually, he made a name for himself, developing his glorious, gravelly voice and his boogie guitar style, with its insistent and mesmerizing rhythm. John Lee's refusal to be constrained to the traditional twelve-bar blues format singled him out, and in 1948 he signed to a tiny record company, who leased his recordings to a much bigger label – Modern. Jackpot! His first single for Modern, 'Boogie Chillen', sold more than a million copies. John Lee Hooker was suddenly a star.

FOOT TAPPER

John Lee accompanied himself on these early recordings, on guitar and foot! He would stamp his foot on the studio floor, and producer Bernie Besmen would record the results. Besmen became irritated by John Lee's habit of moonlighting for other record labels under various pseudonyms, such as John Lee Cooker and Texas Slim. They parted company, but not before another million-seller, 'I'm In The Mood', in 1951.

'The Healer' 1989
'The Ultimate Collection' 1991
'Mr Lucky' 1991
'The Legendary Modern Recordings' 1994, recorded 1948–54
'The Early Years' 1994
'The Very Best Of John Lee Hooker' 1995, recorded 1948–87
'Chill Out' 1995
'Don't Look Back' 1997

LATE BUT SWEET SUCCESS

After 40 years of hard work, most musicians would think about retiring, but not John Lee Hooker. He had his biggest successes in the late 1980s and '90s, with the albums 'The Healer', 'Chill Out' and 'Don't Look Back'. He was still thrilling audiences just weeks before his death in June 2001, aged 80.

Bonnie Raitt appears on John Lee's 1989 album 'The Healer'.

THE BLUES BROTHERS

Released in 1980, 'The Blues Brothers' movie has attracted a cult following over the years. John Belushi and Dan Aykroyd star as brothers Jake and Elwood, who reunite their blues band to raise money to save an orphanage. The plot is flimsy, to say the least. But never mind – the film contains some stunning music, with contributions from guest musicians John Lee Hooker, Aretha Franklin, James Brown, Cab Calloway and Ray Charles. Today, countless Blues Brothers tribute bands keep the spirit of the blues alive, all over the world.

Dan Aykroyd (left) and John Belushi.

ELMORE JAMES

Apart from being an inspiration to thousands of slide guitarists, Elmore James will always be remembered for one of the most memorable riffs in blues history – a riff is a short, repeated musical hook in a song. Countless blues bands all over the world have played the unforgettable, pulverising introduction to 'Dust My Broom'. Many musicians would say that learning that riff is part of your apprenticeship, if you want to take the blues seriously.

LISTENING AND LEARNING

Elmore James was born in that fertile breeding ground for blues performers, Mississippi, in 1918. He learned his craft in the same way as so many others had before him, by listening to the many travelling musicians who played in clubs, at parties and on the streets. Of course, to be a successful performer you had stand out from the crowd and offer something a little different.

BLUES GOES ELECTRIC

Elmore bought an electric guitar in the mid 1940s, when the instrument was still in its infancy. He realized its potential immediately. You could cut right through the noise of a raucous crowd, and produce all sorts of effects by cranking up the volume, creating distortion and feedback. Coupled with that, Elmore decided to play slide guitar to add to the drama. Also known as 'bottleneck', this technique involves using a piece of pipe, or the neck of a bottle, placed over one of the fingers of the left hand, and tuning the guitar's strings to a chord. The slide is then dragged across the strings, creating a wonderful, fluid sound.

BRIAN JONES

Like so many other Mississippi bluesmen, Elmore James had a huge impact on white musicians in the 1960s. Founder member of the Rolling Stones, Brian Jones, was such a big fan that he used the stage name Elmo Lewis for a time. Brian was himself a fine slide guitarist – just listen to the Stones' 'Little Red Rooster' or 'No Expectations' from the 'Beggars Banquet' album to hear Elmore James's influence.

Brian Jones did much to popularize the slide guitar.

Elmore James certainly didn't invent this technique – 'Dust my Broom' was recorded by, amongst others, Robert Johnson – but he perfected and honed this style, and wrote and recorded some classic blues songs, using it to great effect. Luckily, he recorded prolifically, though he never stayed with one record company for long. The lure of another advance payment was too strong, and the fact that he might be contracted to another label didn't seem to worry him!

CLASSIC COMPOSITIONS

Charging around the South in his new car, and playing regularly on Sonny Boy Williamson's 'King Biscuit Time' radio show, Elmore rapidly built up an enthusiastic following, helped in no small measure by the release of some of the best blues records of all time – 'The Sky Is Crying', 'It Hurts Me Too' and 'Shake Your Moneymaker' are just three examples. Sadly, Elmore suffered from serious heart problems, and died in Chicago aged 45 years.

Elmore James and one of his many fans in the 1950s.

ROBERT JOHNSON

Robert Johnson is universally acknowledged to be one of the most important blues performers to have ever lived. But he certainly didn't enjoy fame and fortune during his lifetime, which was tragically cut short when he was just 27 years of age.

'The Complete Recordings' 1990, recorded 1936–7

'King Of The Delta Blues' 1999

COUNTRY BLUES

Robert Johnson was born in 1911 in Mississippi. From a very early age, he listened avidly to the blues musicians wandering from town to town in the deep South. This was true 'country' blues – traditional work songs, with a battered guitar or well-worn harmonica for accompaniment.

Singer and guitarist Steve Miller was hugely influenced by Robert Johnson.

MASTER OF THE GUITAR

Robert Johnson was quick to learn, and rapidly developed a guitar technique which to this day baffles listeners who listen closely to his (all too few) recordings. At times you would swear that you were hearing not one, but two guitarists accompanying his quavery but hugely emotional singing.

The Rolling Stones recorded Johnson's 'Love In Vain' in 1969.

CREAM

The leading British blues band of the 1960s was Cream. Each member was a virtuoso on his chosen instrument – Eric Clapton on guitar, Ginger Baker on drums and Jack Bruce on bass guitar, harmonica and vocals. Cream only lasted for two years, between 1966 and '68, but they recorded four superb albums. The highlight of their double album 'Wheels Of Fire' is a blistering version of Robert Johnson's 'Crossroads', recorded live in San Francisco. Many listeners think the song features Eric Clapton's best-ever guitar solo.

Eric Clapton, Ginger Baker and Jack Bruce.

A DEVIL OF A TALENT

A colourful and enduring myth exists to explain exactly how Johnson acquired this impressive skill – a pact with the Devil, no less! Is is said that he met with the Devil himself at a remote crossroads, who granted him his genius in return for his eternal soul. Well, you can believe that if you choose, but what is in no doubt is his enormous talent. He managed somehow to combine traditional country blues with the more urgent, dramatic sounds which were emerging from the cities which he visited.

THE LEGEND BEGINS

Robert Johnson's songs were often sad, haunting tales which reflected his restless and financially unrewarding lifestyle. He only ever recorded 41 tracks, in Antonio and Dallas between 1936 and 1937. But the end came in 1938, when he was given a poisoned drink in a Mississippi club, probably by the husband of a woman he had made advances towards. After several days' illness, Robert Johnson died.

B.B. KING

Many listeners consider B.B. King to be the best lead guitarist in the world. Yet this remarkable blues veteran freely admits that he cannot play chords. Nor can he sing and play at the same time. Certainly he is one of the hardest working and most accomplished blues performers of all time – 'King of the blues'.

'Together Live' 1987, with Bobby Bland
'Indianola Mississippi Seeds' 1989, recorded 1970
'Blues Is King' 1990
'Singin' The Blues'/The Blues' 1993, recorded 1951–61
'Live At The Regal' 1997, recorded 1964
'His Definitive Greatest Hits' 1999

A SOULFUL SINGER

B.B. King possesses a powerful and rich voice which might have been well-suited to soul, gospel or even operatic music. In addition, his clean, expressive and deeply emotional guitar-playing is the envy of virtually every blues guitarist in the world.

EARLY INFLUENCES

Riley 'Blues Boy' King was born near Indianola, Mississippi in 1925. As a teenager, he was heavily influenced by gospel music, but he also revered guitarist T. Bone Walker's subtle string-bending technique. Memphis, Tennessee, not Chicago, was B.B.'s first port of call after a spell in the army. In 1949 his career took an unexpected turn – he became a successful radio disc jockey.

THE OTHER KINGS

B.B. is not the only blues star called King. Albert King was born in Indianola, close to B.B.'s birthplace. Journalists assumed that they must be related (particularly as B.B.'s father was called Albert), and neither bluesman denied this false rumour. Albert mastered the guitar, despite the fact that he was left-handed and strung the instrument upside down. Texan Freddy King moved to Chicago in the 1950s and recorded prolifically. Rock star Leon Russell signed him to his Shelter label in the early '70s and turned him into a superstar. Sadly, Freddy died young, after a heart attack on stage in Dallas, on Christmas Day 1976.

Freddy King pictured shortly before his death.

Albert King with a personalized guitar.

A LIFE ON THE ROAD

But performing was his first love, and it was inevitable that he would come to the attention of a record company. When he signed to Modern in the early 1950s, B.B. King found success – at a price. He had to tour relentlessly in order to bring in the income to support himself and his band. He was still performing over 300 concerts per year into his seventies.

LIVE AT THE REGAL

In 1961, B.B. signed a contract with ABC. In '64, the company decided to record him in the environment in which he excels – on stage in front of an enthusiastic audience. The resulting album, 'Live At The Regal', is hailed by many critics as the finest live blues album of all time. B.B. recorded more excellent albums in front of live audiences – one audience the inmates of Cook County Jail!

A STRING OF HITS

B.B.'s long run of hits began in 1969, when 'The Thrill Is Gone' entered the Top 20, and he often collaborates with younger musicians. A recent partner was Eric Clapton on the Grammy award-winning album 'Riding With The King', recorded in 2000.

B.B. King in the studio with Peter Green of Fleetwood Mac, himself a superb blues guitarist.

A live performance with Bono of U2.

JIMMY REED

Jimmy Reed was one of the biggest influences on younger blues artists, notably the Rolling Stones. He also played a major part in starting one of the most important blues record labels, Vee-Jay. Yet his reputation is often overshadowed by other Mississippi blues stars, such as John Lee Hooker and B.B. King.

VEE-JAY IS BORN

Born in 1925, Jimmy Reed moved to Chicago from Mississippi in the mid 1940s and teamed up with the excellent guitar-player Eddie Taylor. Aged around 26 years, Jimmy and Eddie went along to the home of urban blues, the legendary Chess Records in Chicago – and were turned down. Undeterred, Jimmy went across town to a record shop owned by Vivian Carter and her husband Jimmy Brackent, and begged them to help him cut a disc. The results were issued on Chance, but when that label went out of business, Vee-Jay was founded. For Jimmy, it was the start of a recording career which would see the release of such classic records as 'You Don't Have To Go', 'Bright Lights, Big City', 'Baby Please Don't Go', 'Hush Hush', 'Big Boss Man' and many more.

Jimmy Reed, with his harmonica around his neck.

MAMA KNOWS BEST

Jimmy owed a lot of his success to his talented and supportive wife, Mama Reed. She wrote most of the lyrics, and helped Jimmy (who couldn't read or write) by quietly prompting him, a line at a time, in the studio. He achieved chart success in the R&B *and* popular listings, no mean feat for a blues performer, although Jimmy never received the income he deserved from his huge record sales.

Jimmy was always well turned out on stage.

ONE OF A KIND

It was the laid-back, slurred, almost gruff delivery of his songs that characterized Jimmy's work, punctuated by sharp, high-pitched harmonica licks – another of his trademarks. Eddie Taylor's unfussy guitar work also contributed to his unique sound. But sadly, Jimmy was not able to sustain his career for as long as he deserved to. Like so many other performers before and since, he turned to alcohol to relieve the hours of tedium on the road.

BEGINNING OF THE END

Jimmy's career suffered a real setback when Eddie Taylor stopped playing with him. His unobtrusive contribution to the sound had been crucial to its success. Jimmy was left high and dry, and he never again attained the artistic heights of his previous work. He continued recording and touring, but sadly his illnesses took their toll. Jimmy Reed died in 1976, aged just 51.

MEMPHIS SLIM

Like Jimmy Reed, pianist Memphis Slim was one of the first artists to record with the newly-formed Vee-Jay label. Slim was born in Memphis, and carved out a career as Big Bill Broonzy's invaluable accompanist. After a tour of Europe with bassist Willie Dixon in 1962, he settled in Paris, where he lived until his death in 1988.

Memphis Slim was revered in his adopted Paris.

BESSIE SMITH

Very few recording artists can claim to have sold over three-quarters of a million copies of their debut single. It is quite extraordinary, then, that a relatively unknown singer from the deep South of the United States could achieve that milestone back in 1923. It is particularly impressive when you consider that the market-place for such artists was restricted to the black population, and the massive national radio air-play, enjoyed by pop stars today, simply wasn't available. But this was no ordinary performer. This was Bessie Smith, the 'Empress of the blues'.

RAGS TO RICHES

Born in Chattanooga, Tennessee in 1894, Bessie was orphaned at a very early age. Life was tough, but with her awesome voice, she found that she could earn nickels and dimes by singing on street corners. Her's wasn't the only talent in the family. Her brother Clarence joined the fearsome 'Ma' Rainey in her travelling show, and Bessie soon followed suit. After her apprenticeship with 'Ma', Bessie went solo. Her debut, 'Downhearted Blues', was soon followed by the classic ''Tain't Nobody's Business If I Do'. The publicity she received from these huge hits meant that she could demand fees of between one and three thousand dollars per week – a fortune in those days.

Bessie starred in 'Pansy' on Broadway.

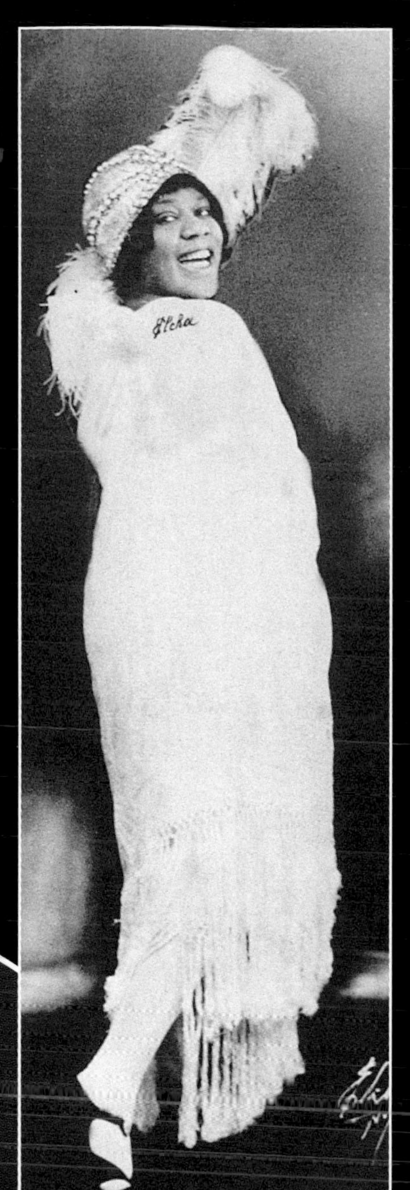

SONGS WITH LOUIS

Life seemed rosy, and her collaboration with another superstar, Louis Armstrong, put the icing on the cake. Bessie Smith was a star, the most successful female blues singer ever. New York's Broadway stage beckoned. She had just recorded the beautiful song 'Nobody Knows You When You're Down And Out', when disaster struck.

THE CURTAIN FALLS

Following the Wall Street Crash, theatres closed all over the United States – nobody could afford to visit them. At a stroke, Bessie's lucrative career vanished. Reduced to singing for a few dollars in cheap nightclubs, and increasingly dependent on drugs and alcohol, her decline was as spectacular as her rise to fame had been. But although Bessie was down, she wasn't out. In 1933, she recorded with Benny Goodman, and seemed to be inching her way back to her former glory. Sadly, though, Bessie was killed in a car crash in 1937.

THE WALL STREET CRASH

The 1929 collapse of the New York stock market, or Wall Street Crash, was one of the most devastating events of the 20th century. Many experts considered the value of public companies (their stock prices) to be grossly overpriced, and they began to sell their shares in the market. This caused panic as countless investors followed suit. Stock prices tumbled, numerous businesses closed down and millions of people became unemployed all over the Western world. The Great Depression that followed caused misery and hardship throughout the 1930s.

There was mayhem on Wall Street, New York's financial centre, when stocks collapsed in 1929.

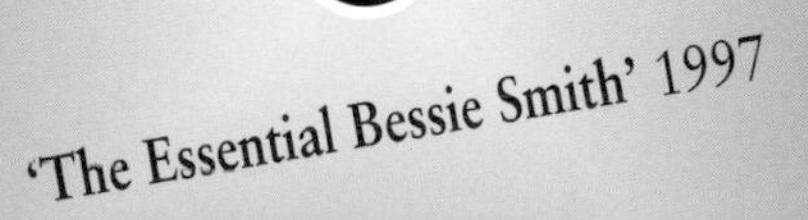

Bessie was killed in Clarksdale, Mississippi.

MUDDY WATERS

One of the roles of the American Library of Congress is to record for posterity the history of American music, art and other areas of culture. Researchers record interviews with performers, writers, historians – in fact anybody who can help them to construct this gigantic body of information.

A JOURNEY DOWN SOUTH

In 1941, Library of Congress folklorist Alan Lomax travelled to Mississippi, to research 'country' blues music, usually performed by solo musicians roaming the South in search of a few dollars. He was particularly interested in Robert Johnson's work, and his trail led him to the primitive home of McKinley Morganfield, better known as Muddy Waters.

MUSICAL HERITAGE

Lomax immediately realized that he had stumbled upon a giant amongst blues players. Muddy, by then 26 years old, was a farm labourer, who had been playing blues music for over 15 years. Lomax hastily recorded him on his trusty government tape recorder. Muddy performed several songs, including an interesting (and perhaps surprising) song praising his farm boss! Lomax was back in 1942 to record more material, but Muddy would not be found in the deep South for much longer. In 1943, like so many bluesmen, he made the trek to Chicago.

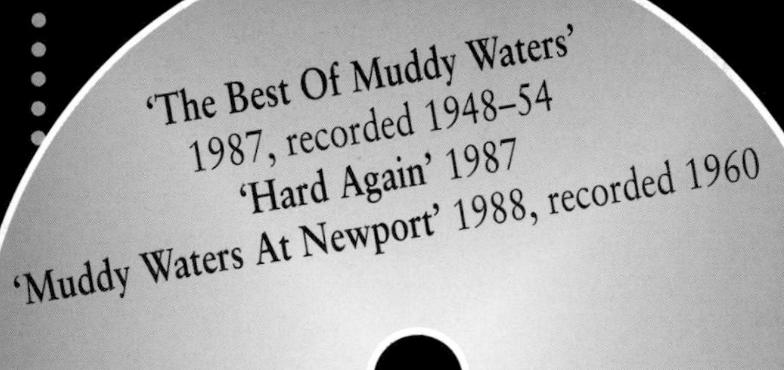

MAKING A NAME FOR HIMSELF

Muddy Waters hit town, and started a day job driving a truck. By night, he played in clubs and at parties, powerfully accompanying himself on amplified slide guitar. He worked for a while with Big Bill Broonzy and quickly established a reputation around town. Muddy also met bass-player and songwriter Willie Dixon who would have a huge influence on his career. Muddy quickly came to the notice of Leonard Chess, owner of the Chess label, and his career took off.

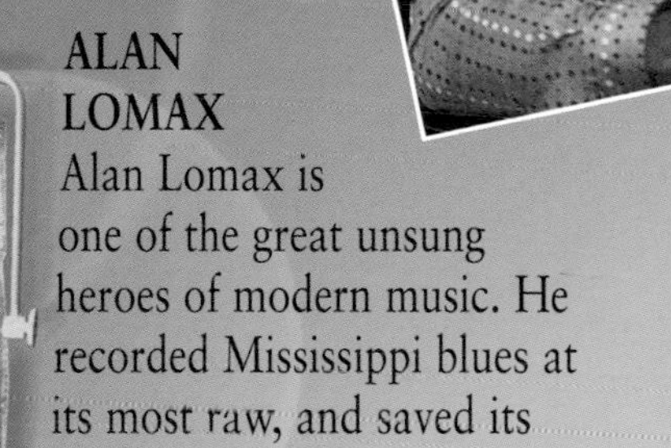

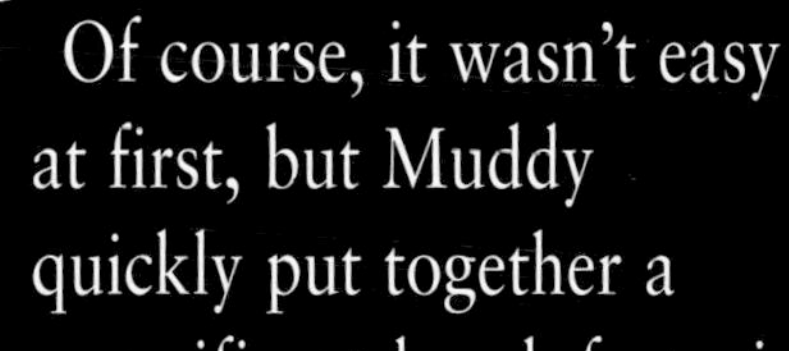

Muddy and his Fender Telecaster electric guitar.

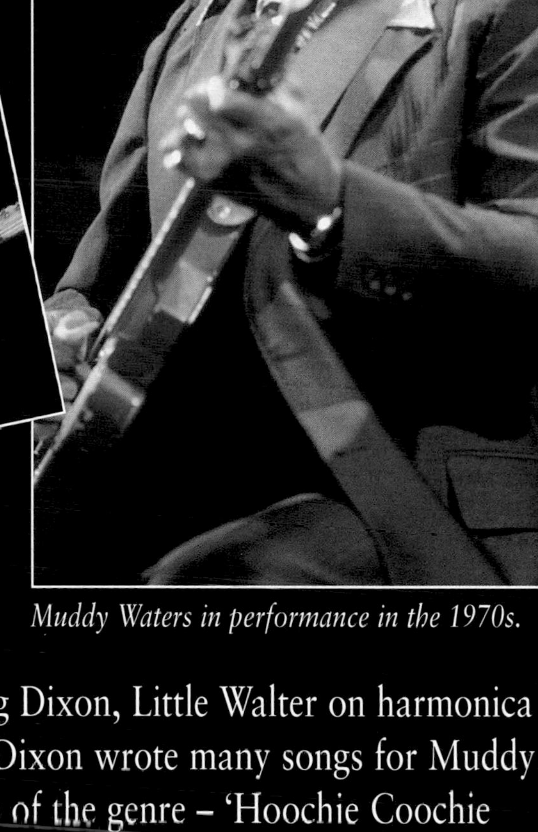

Muddy Waters in performance in the 1970s.

Of course, it wasn't easy at first, but Muddy quickly put together a magnificent band, featuring Dixon, Little Walter on harmonica and Otis Spann on piano. Dixon wrote many songs for Muddy that would become classics of the genre – 'Hoochie Coochie Man', 'I Just Want To Make Love To You' and a blues anthem if ever there was one, 'I've Got My Mojo Working'.

ALAN LOMAX

Alan Lomax is one of the great unsung heroes of modern music. He recorded Mississippi blues at its most raw, and saved its traditions from being lost forever. Without Lomax's detective-work, there might have been no blues explosion in the 1960s, no Beatles or Rolling Stones and, in turn, most of the pop acts of today would not exist.

Alan Lomax – saviour of the blues.

AN IDOL TO YOUNGER MUSICIANS

By the 1970s, Muddy Waters and his band were international stars, and Muddy loved every minute of it. His recording career was given some much-needed help by guitarist Johnny Winter, who enthusiastically produced some stunning albums with Muddy on the Blue Sky label, featuring some wonderful re-recordings of his previous hits. In 1981, Muddy was joined on stage by the Rolling Stones, who took their name from his first Chess single, 'Rollin' Stone'. Muddy died in 1983, and the world lost one of the greatest blues performers of all time.

SONNY BOY WILLIAMSON

The first Sonny Boy Williamson.

The first question must be 'which one?'. For there were two harmonica players who used the name, both talented in their different ways. Let's start with Sonny Boy Williamson I.

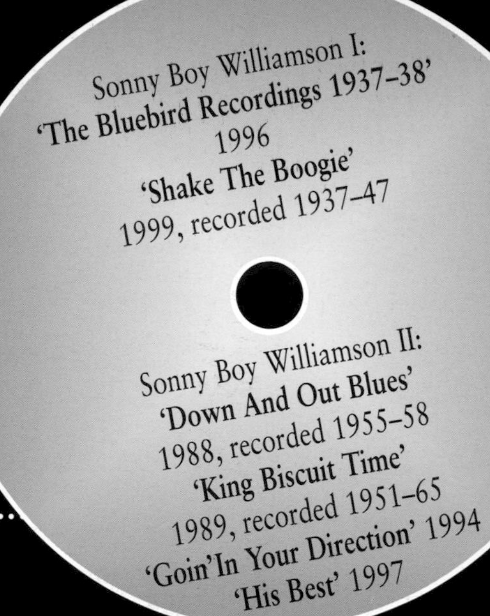

HARP HERO

His real name was John Lee Williamson. Born in Jackson, Tennessee in 1914, he moved to Memphis in his twenties. The harmonica was not yet accepted as a credible lead instrument in blues ensembles, playing more of a supporting role for front line performers. But Williamson wanted to thrust his harp to the forefront, and vigorously developed his own technique, playing melody lines and sophisticated solos.

Sonny Boy Williamson II.

Sonny Boy Williamson II had a moody personality.

A CAREER CUT SHORT

Williamson struck lucky in 1937, when he teamed up with musical giants Big Joe Williams on vocals and Robert Nighthawk on guitar to make his first recordings. These included the songs 'Good Morning Little Schoolgirl' and 'Sugar Mama Blues'. He would go on to record and perform with other great artists such as Willie Dixon and Muddy Waters. Tragically, his life was cut short when he was murdered outside a nightclub in 1948.

MAN OF MYSTERY

The second Sonny Boy Williamson's real name could have been Rice Miller, or Alex Ford, or Willie Williams – take your pick! Nobody knows where or when he was born, but we do know that by 1930, he was working as a musician under the name Little Boy Blue, and that he probably played with Robert Johnson. When the first Sonny Boy was murdered, he took his name, claiming to be 'the original Sonny Boy'. Although his fellow musicians still referred to him as Rice Miller, nobody else seemed to notice!

FATHER FIGURE

Sonny Boy enjoyed his greatest successes in the 1960s when he came to Britain, and bands such as the Animals and the Yardbirds fell over themselves to play with him. He died in 1965, the last link between ancient and modern blues.

Sonny Boy Williamson II (centre) was a regular on the 'King Biscuit Time' radio show in the '40s.

BLUES HARP

There can't be many blues singers who don't also play the harmonica, or harp. Howlin' Wolf, Jimmy Reed and white musicians, such as Robert Plant of Led Zeppelin and Mick Jagger of the Rolling Stones, have all complemented their vocals with the harp. It has always been a popular instrument amongst blues singers – it's cheap and portable – but don't let anyone tell you it's easy to master. Both Sonny Boy Williamsons, for example, spent years practising and perfecting their style.

Robert Plant on the harp.

HOWLIN' WOLF

Howlin' Wolf didn't get his nickname without good reason – a feature of his awesome singing style was his howling, just like an injured, angry wolf! He could be terrifying to watch. A huge man, aggression was never far from the surface, and woe betide any sideman or audience member who crossed him. You didn't argue with the Wolf – one look at those fists, the size of small hams, would frighten the most courageous critic.

THE SINGING FARMER

Chester Arthur Burnett was born in 1910 in West Point, Mississippi, a small farming community. Indeed, although he played with Robert Johnson and Sonny Boy Williamson II from his late teens, he remained a farmer until around 1940, and he never did learn to read, write or count. Like B.B. King, Howlin' Wolf headed to Memphis rather than Chicago to find fame and fortune, and like B.B., became a radio disc jockey. His vocal talents were discovered by Ike Turner.

CHESS SUCCESS

In 1951, the Wolf cut a disc at the Sun studios in Memphis. Turner was astounded by the sheer power and pain in his astonishing voice. A contract with Chess Records soon followed.

Howlin' Wolf was built more like a bear than a wolf!

A FEARSOME BLUESMAN

Howlin' Wolf was a very difficult man to work with, but several notable sidemen stuck with him, including Hubert Sumlin and the man who played on more Chess sides than any other musician, bass-player and writer Willie Dixon. The Wolf deeply distrusted Dixon, jealous of the songwriting royalties Dixon earned from tracks such as 'Little Baby', 'Wang Dang Doodle' and the classic 'Spoonful'. It was the hurricane force of his vocal delivery, with its chilling wails and howls that made Howlin' Wolf the unique bluesman that he was. He often toured Britain, scaring the pants off the hapless young musicians who accompanied him.

Howlin' Wolf also played the harmonica.

LEONARD CHESS

The legendary Chess Records was co-founded by two brothers, Leonard and Philip Chess, who had emigrated to Chicago from their native Poland as children. They took over the Aristocrat label in 1950, renaming it Chess. Their roster of artists represents the blues aristocracy – Howlin' Wolf, Jimmy Rogers, Little Walter, Muddy Waters, Bobby Bland, Buddy Guy, Otis Rush, Sonny Boy Williamson, Bo Diddley, Etta James, Little Milton, Rufus Thomas and Chuck Berry all recorded for the Chess label.

Leonard Chess, shortly before his death in 1969.

FRIENDS IN THE UK

The Wolf travelled to London in 1971, to record with a superstar line-up of British musicians, including Eric Clapton. The resulting 'London Howlin' Wolf Sessions' is a classic. His final years were clouded by ill-health and a car crash. He died in 1976.

GAZETTEER

'Ma' Rainey was a hugely talented, loud and risqué singer.

People have been singing and playing the blues for the best part of a century now, and the influence of those wandering Mississippi musicians has stretched all over the world. The musicians on the previous pages are just some of the major figures in blues. The following artists have also played a part in shaping this unique musical genre.

Stevie Ray Vaughan (right) was more famous than his brother Jimmy (left).

INVENTOR OF THE BLUES?

Gertrude Pridgett became 'Ma' Rainey, when she married 'Pa' Rainey, a comedian, whose speciality was stuffing a saucer into his mouth! 'Ma' claimed to have invented the word 'blues'. Perhaps, but what is beyond doubt is her stunning vocal technique, even heard 80 years later.

BLUES BASS-PLAYERS

As well as being Howlin' Wolf's longtime partner, Willie Dixon was a fine bass-player and songwriter. His compositions include the Rolling Stones' hit 'Little Red Rooster'. Another bass-master was Eddie Taylor, who joined Jimmy Reed and John Lee Hooker on the fledgling Vee-Jay label.

Willie Dixon plays a double bass, not an electric bass guitar.

Eddie Taylor was one of the first artists on Vee-Jay records.

RHYTHM AND BLUES

The closest relative to the blues is its faster and livelier cousin, rhythm and blues (R&B). Its greatest exponent was Chuck Berry, still wowing audiences into his seventies, with his original vocal and guitar style. His songs include 'Maybelline', 'Sweet Little Sixteen' and 'No Particular Place To Go' (which he is said to have written during a spell in jail!).

Chuck Berry always plays a Gibson guitar.

John Mayall (far left) with his Bluesbreakers, including Eric Clapton (second from right) and John McVie (far right).

GODFATHER OF BRITISH BLUES

Manchester-born keyboard-player John Mayall has been flying the flag for blues since the 1950s. His band, the Bluesbreakers, variously featured esteemed guitarists Eric Clapton, Peter Green of Fleetwood Mac and Mick Taylor of the Rolling Stones. Now an American citizen, John still tours the world with a new generation of Bluesbreakers.

George Thorogood leads the Destroyers.

BLUES BROTHERS

Stevie Ray Vaughan was the undisputed king of Texan blues in the 1980s. His blisteringly fast guitar sounded like nothing that had come before. Just check out his 'Live Alive' CD, or the studio album 'Texas Flood'. He also teamed up with his brother Jimmy to make up the Vaughan Brothers. Tragically, Stevie's career was cut short in 1990, when he was killed in an air crash, along with a number of colleagues, while touring with Eric Clapton.

BLUES DESTROYER

Delaware guitarist George Thorogood has been leading his band the Destroyers for three decades. An excellent slide-guitarist, his heavy blues style came to wide attention in 1985, when he jammed with Albert Collins at the Live Aid concert in Philadelphia. Artists such as George are working hard to keep the blues alive and well. Let's hope it stays that way for a very long time!

INDEX

PHOTOGRAPHIC CREDITS Abbreviations: t-top, m-middle, b-bottom, r-right, l-left, c-centre.

Cover m, 22tl & 23mr - Hulton Archive. Cover bl, 16tl, 17tr (Deltahaze) Cover bm, 5tr, 7mr, 8bl, 9mr, 10mr & bl, 11br, 14br, 18br, 19tl, 20mr, 20-21, 21br, 24tl, 24-25, 25tr, 26br, 28 both, 30bl (David Redfern) Cover br, 10tl, 12ml, 12-13, 30tr (Robert Knight) 3, 6 both, 7tl & br (Gerrit Schilp) 4-5, 8tl, 14tl, 16b, 17ml, 18tl, 20tl, 21tl, 22-23, 23tl, 25bl, 26tl & ml, 29mr, 31mr (Michael Ochs Archives) 9tl (Mick Hutson) 9bl (Leon Morris) 11t (Nicky J. Sims) 12tl, 29bl (Redferns) 13ml, 25ml (Richie Aaron) 13br, 15bl, 27b (Glenn A. Baker Archives) 15br (Gems) 16-17 (RB) 19ml (Dave Ellis) 19bl (Keith Morris) 19br (Bob King) 23br, 30tl, 30br (Max Jones Files) 27mr (Jon Super) 31bl (Patrick Ford) - Redferns. 31tl - The Kobal Collection.

Sound Trackers

Blues

David West Children's Books
7 Princeton Court
55 Felsham Road
London SW15 1AZ

Designer: Rob Shone
Picture Research: Fiona Thorne
Editor: James Pickering

First published in Great Britain in 2002 by
Heinemann Library, Halley Court, Jordan Hill, Oxford OX2 8EJ, a division of
Reed Educational and Professional Publishing Limited.

OXFORD MELBOURNE AUCKLAND
JOHANNESBURG BLANTYRE GABORONE
IBADAN PORTSMOUTH (NH) USA CHICAGO

06 05 04 03 02
10 9 8 7 6 5 4 3 2 1

ISBN 0 431 09110 2 (HB)
ISBN 0 431 09117 X (PB)

British Library Cataloguing in Publication Data

Brunning, Bob
Blues. - (Soundtrackers)
1. Blues (Music) - Juvenile literature
2. Blues musicians - Juvenile literature
I. Title
781.6'43

Printed and bound in Italy